Piano Keys out of Breath

Running in the Wind

Kane Benjamin Crookes

Grosvenor House
Publishing Limited

All rights reserved
Copyright © Kane Benjamin Crookes, 2025

The right of Kane Benjamin Crookes to be identified as the author
of this work has been asserted in accordance with Section 78
of the Copyright, Designs and Patents Act 1988

The book cover is copyright to Kane Benjamin Crookes

This book is published by
Grosvenor House Publishing Ltd
Link House
140 The Broadway, Tolworth, Surrey, KT6 7HT.
www.grosvenorhousepublishing.co.uk

This book is sold subject to the conditions that it shall not, by way of
trade or otherwise, be lent, resold, hired out or otherwise circulated
without the author's or publisher's prior consent in any form of
binding or cover other than that in which it is published and
without a similar condition including this condition being
imposed on the subsequent purchaser.

This book is a work of fiction. Any resemblance to
people or events, past or present, is purely coincidental.

A CIP record for this book
is available from the British Library

ISBN 978-1-83615-217-0

Preface

I set myself a challenge of writing as many poems as possible throughout the autumn and wintertime. I did this, as I aim to highlight my day-to-day thought processes to my readers, giving the collection a more intimate feel. This was done through, like with my last, a series of free verse and haiku, some of which capture the mere essence and sensory details of nature, for there was more focus on thought and image rather than language. Most, however, aim to convey the supernatural, using the fact that I strived to showcase nature as something other or apparitional.

I was inspired by poets such as Christina Rossetti, Matsuo Basho, Matthew Arnold, Brian Sneeden, Luke Levi, G.K. Chesterton, Jericho Brown and Ezra Pound. I was captivated by the way in which Rossetti explores themes of resurrection and the afterlife in her poem, *After Death* (1862), whilst developing a confused aspect of love and loss. She personifies the, I quote, 'rushes, rosemary and may' which seem to overtake the motionless body with her use of the preposition 'on' rather than 'in'.

The poems in this collection also explore the themes of love and loss; in this case, I'd like to consider them as ones with series of layers. As well as the moon, you will also find that cherries have been frequently used, especially in haiku. Unlike my first book, haiku in this collection does not rely on the 5-7-5 syllable count, which was done to showcase nature somewhat having control over the poems, as well as the fleetingness of thought.

The first three pages of the collection will introduce poems written by my friends, Elisha Singh, Megan Hall and Chanel Ricketts, as I want to bring a sense of belonging in the collection and give my friends the opportunity to share their creative endeavours. Also included are my eccentric doodles on a couple of photographs taken by my best friend, Ava, during her travels through Japan in January 2023. These are, of course, followed by haiku written by me.

On a final note: there is a childlike innocence expressed throughout the lines, some of which can be educational. This is due to tailoring my poems to a younger audience for my Reading Children's Literature module; however, I've found that my poems have always had a childlike innocence that creates a feeling of longing. But I hope you all – as my audience – enjoy the imagery in this collection with which I hope you can resonate.

'Hyop' *animal*

'Red pain of pleasure bleaches the sheep's canvas.

    Bitten cherries poisoned the ravenous wolves. Go, escape this death!'

By Elisha Singh.

A doodle on Ava Crowther's photograph of pink blossoms
'Pink blossoms,
Are hanging
I feed them tulips'
A haiku.

'Fine China,
I take a dip into your tea'

'Other than I didn't ask for sugar
I didn't ask for a spoon
Yet you still put them in
Sweet taste, distasteful face
I don't want your tea'

By Chanel Darwent Ricketts.

A doodle on Ava Crowther's photograph, Osaka, Japan
'In Osaka the
Tree was waving,
Behind the deer'
A haiku.

A doodle on my photograph of a
tree, Manchester, February 2024
'A petal on the branch
Was hung out
To dry'
A haiku.

'humanity is not human'

'and so the lion lived amongst the lamb.
clasped by the moon,
white claws bloomed and
hunger sang.

stem away from primitive beginnings,
sinister instincts,
humanity ceases,
hallows haunt the breeze
that pleads,
needy to
die.
blows to the dark side.

humanity is not human – at least not in the moonlight.'

By Megan Elizabeth Hall.

'Pale Leaves'

Veins like ink, burst, and
      spill
          Over pale leaves—
The little capes circled,
Over,

      Like *webs*, span like spinning tops

The black sun, shines,
      Branches smiled, enigmas

'The Lake'

White paint

    Spilled

Onto the midnight curtain

    The moon
And pastel-yellow petals are added, to twinkle
On top to be

Stirred with sticks

'The Print'

Noir, like a forest

      Sage

Maud—
Strewn flower petals
      For her hat, dress

Sewn, daisy
The print—

'Wands of Ivory'

Water
     drips

 Trickles
    Wands of
 Ivory, for

Wishful, dandelions

Greyish, a white
     Feather flew,

Let the blue—

'The Milky Way'

The Milky Way, yesterday,
On which day will you
Grin in the sun?

'Dewdrops'

On a leaf,
In which dewdrops sleep
During the night,
I cannot see

'Leaf on a Stream'

Leaf—
 On a stream

Floats
    Like a blanket
    Placed onto fire

Spells from the blue—

'The Ash Railway'

And the knittings became
ghostlike,
Was the moon;

Living, is the
Petal, in the birdhouse;

The ash railway

'Teeth Fed on the Window'

A thousand frosts'
Teeth fed on the window
Like galactic stars

'Blood Spills Over the Sky'

Blood spills over the sky
Like an *abstract* work of art
Like *pieces* to a puddle, that
Floats the finest feather
On which I shall sit—stare at
Earthly autumnal *colours*

'Bleeding'

The red bough, hangs
A line of rubies
Merrymaking in the leaves—
Bleeding rich blood

'The Moon Tarnished'

The moon's blood vessels
Burst, and dressed himself
Blush red, like hell's devil
On which clung, swung,
Like heaven's child—a swing,
For he was dressed—*bandages,*
And the bed—healed, *managed,*
The wine spilled; *the moon* tarnished

'Running out of Breath'

And the moon slept above
Like a thousand spherical
Piano keys—the snowlike daisy
Running—out of breath

'There's the fog'

There's the fog—
Like smoke
Choking the blue;
I light my own,
The sun's throne

'Spiders Hung'

A fog-laden hillside—
Nighttime, with which the
Moon paints the grass—
Blackened—like spiders,
Building a web—hung:
The red bough, air-stirred

'Black Paper'

On the rooftops
Like a child's room
And the black paper
Covered in fresh glitter
In love—the drawn moon,
And the sunset—after noon

'Pale-Apple Skies'

Pale-apple skies
Like a poisonous Ivy
Growing like bubbles,
Wishful dandelions:

'A Giant Claw'

The palm tree, stroked
The sun like wishful wands
Like a giant claw
Gnawing at the seams—
My whitest collar

'The Greek Moon'

The Greek moon
Put on his yellow raincoat
Floats on the stream
And the branches sprawled, out
Like arms of ink-smeared
Children who crawled

'The Crystal'

The clouds and the
Sun created the brightest
Crystal

'The Sea Ran'

And the sea ran,
Crashing over the moon
By which it was dressed in
Its freshest salts,
The cut-out snowflakes

'The Night's Palm Tree'

The nighttime palm
Like silhouetted
Spines, torn from the
Skeleton—*blowing in*
The wind—*waving at*
Me

'Gasped for Breath'

The sunflowers in the basket
On wheels, gasped
For breath

'The British Sun'

The British sun, dipped in snow
Like a sheep, over the moon,
Hung, there, the afternoon

'White Gloves'

Green wine held by the sun
Poured onto white sugar
Covering the tea *leaves*
Hanging *like white gloves*

'Silver Mist'

The pearls of morning dew
Vocals of silver mist
Swung like nooses, and
Dragging, lime grass

'Chimera'

The golden petal,
Amidst,
Choking silver mist—

'Resurrection'

I write myself a *hokku*:
The *moon*, *white flowers*, the *snow*
Nighttime, aluminium tapestries
Resting like deathbeds
For suns in which they lay
Post-decomposition

'There was a Tunnel'

And there was a tunnel
From which pine trees hung
And where deers stood—
Sickened jewels, passersby

'The Moon and the Devil'

The sun and leaves
Red wine spills
The moon and the devil

'A Red Bough Waves'

A red bough waves
On a crisp royal canvas
Where leaves, blooded hands,
Just covered in paint

'Purple Vine Leaves'

Purple vine leaves
Falling into the puddle
Kissed by red stars
And the swinging moon
Drips from my fingertips

'White Eyes'

Pale leaves painted purple
Like blue to white eyes, of the
Children, in the *sunset*
Crying down *scarlet blood*

'Frostbitten Leaves'

I write with frostbitten leaves,
But those petal-green came forth
For the canvas, to fill the blanks,
Passing through the riverbanks—
Where train tracks smiled, and beyond
The lily on the beck, of which I am fond
Was the sun, smiling down on me
In an outfit: the power cables—
Like Sellotape to a fine tapestry
Resting over the tarmac
For the coffee leaf, staring helplessly

'Stars in their Spheres'

Stars are singing in their spheres,
But in water float like white shirts,
On which buttons smile, for
A while, is the naked leaf, the dirt:
Grows a sick hand like a bud-flower, and
Ghastly figures, under the bower—
Lit up by the moon, the sun, afternoons
Paint a desert-red sky for June—
During which Ivy's dance and smile; for now,
I weave them to clothe the imperial—

'Bud-flower'

White shirt in water
Picked out crystal clear
Are the vines stitched, and
Petals of the bud-flower open
Long-sleeved

'Skeletons Rise'

The moon is a gold petal—
That fell into black water,
And swam across the beck
Upon which skeletons rise

'Whispers'

Stars decay in whispers—
Light, as dawn seeps in

'A Thousand Suns'

Across the yellow river
Like a thousand suns—
Daisies on their cheeks

'Melting Corpses'

Melting corpses in the sun
Spinning around like medicine
Brown swirls like a hypnotism,
And the sun on a delicate string

'Red Leaves'

Red leaves on a canvas
And all those white spaces
At which the rose knocks the window—
All the green places;
A crisp leaf on beds of emeralds,
Dancing through a fine white curtain—
A smile on their faces

'Just Now'

And the sun smiles through webs
Clothing the most vulnerable bough
Dances its lightest leaves, *light winds*
Blow like chestnuts on the path, *just now*

'Hanging'

The moon is on fire
Spitting multicolours
Like magic sparklers
Like Christmas lights
Hanging

'Nature's Finest Song'

The leaves through windowpanes
Turn ivory white for piano keys
To play nature's finest song—
Some notes, to which I don't belong

'Stuck in the Milky Way'

The stars are like fireworks
Unlike in the month of May,
Where the sun stares too long
For now, I'm stuck in the Milky Way

'The Blue Scarf'

The moon wraps up in gold foil
I can see the reflection of my smile
My teeth are gnawing at the seams—
The blue scarf

'The Mist'

The mist on the black bough
Tracing over sharp, wet leaves
Dripping down onto the cobbles
Awakening the crescent moon

'My Pen'

On the canvas,
I put forth my pen,
When the moon smiles

'Black Veil'

The moon wears a black veil
On which stars float down
And stand, the top of the tree—
These silhouettes, are next to me

'The Moon Grins'

A brown fog sweeps in
Engulfing the purple rose;
The moon holds a branch to grin,
And my blood like ice froze

'A Wash of Green'

Tree branches through windowpanes
Show nature, cinematic
Comes forth a wash of green

'Swinging on a String'

The clouds are cotton balls
Soaking up the purple moon
Presenting such anaemic white,
Swinging on a string in the night

'Smothered in Glue'

Wet leaves stuck onto the moon
Like a scrapbook
Smothered in glue, dripping,

'The Berries in White Coats'

If skies were green, and snow
Was gold, the fruits on
The tree cannot be told
The berries in white coats
In wintertime, November colds

'A Red Blazer'

The moon wore a red blazer
Like a poppy, crisp
As apparitions:

'Purple Hands'

The moon, a pool of white blood
Bubbling in the winds
Bring forth purple, sharp hands

'Green Town'

A black bough curled up
Like a serpent in the sun—
Climbs down from the clouds
Walk the silver, green town

'Winter Sound'

The sun smothered in glue
Seeps through the cotton
Wrapped tightly around—
The emeralds, winter sound

'Winter, Come Again'

The moon is a snowball
White as the night became
Pale men walking the road,
Winter, winter come again

'A Blade'

The moon under a bedcover
And falls out, a blade
I am laid aside

'Moonlight'

Moonlight struck the path
With snowflakes, due wrath
Screams, these frosty seams
And daisies frown by all means

'The Red Umbrella'

The red umbrella
Dripping
Cherry blossoms

'Streetlight'

A streetlight had guided me
Towards the sun over there
Laid upon the grass, the mist,
Now I'm tracing over it in the air

'A Wash of White'

I paint a hillside during the night
And stick onto the canvas
Paper stars, to guide the moon,
A wash of white in the afternoon

'The Sun Falls Off'

The pavement is full of stars—
Rise, sticking to my pale face
From which blue petals grow
And the sun falls off the glaze

'Broken Skulls'

The moon engulfed by clouds
Like broken skulls, eating
Their way through the wet soil

'Carriage Wheels'

The crows around the church
Like horse *carriage wheels*
Reel in sweet, blue mist

'Carriage Window'

A yellow river
Washed over the
Carriage window

'Green Leaves'

Green leaves on the wall:
Nature's necklace, glimmering,
Blinding me through windowpanes

'A Basket of Rare Fruit'

A basket full of rare fruit
Pouring out onto the path
Melons on the grass lanes
Smiling beneath white suns
The moon is a watermelon
Dripping with strawberries
Hanging from the doorframe
Washed white like a canvas
Purple grapes for a necklace

'A Red Carpet'

The sun walks, a red carpet
Was the grass, beneath my
Feet, cold and blue spotted
Green, the Ivy's are to weave
Together, the moon's corset

'Cobwebs'

Cobwebs climb my window
For me to wake, and spin
In the sun, kisses the grass,
Wraps around my pale throat
Strawberries for my larynx

'A Wash of Black'

I stick silk-green
Bows onto windowpanes:
Bring forth a wash of black

'A Photo Frame'

The moon is a photo frame
Smiling was those children
I stick silk-green bows onto
And soon falls off is the face

'A Sick Hand'

The moon is a bauble
Comes forth a sick hand
To crush, and snap its pale
Wrist presents the morning lands

'Water's Birthday'

Fire chases green bows on
A string, for Water's birthday
During the nighttime, the rain
Which dances, the holly hedge,
Frost coats to send her to sleep

'Berries'

The holly hedge is starlit:
With a gaping wound
Like a handful of rubies, for
Berries, rolling *down pathways*

'Dew's Handwriting'

Dew's handwriting,
On petalled leaves,
In the morning—

'Disappeared'

The fog stood, a sketchbook
In the tunnel: out of it
Disappeared, the sun

'The Chorus'

And began, the chorus
Turning their faces blue
But they:

'Grass for Spines'

The canvas on which I drew a wreath
Like a thousand hands bleeding,
Reaching to pour onto the grass
For verse, and grass for spines,
Extracted for joyous, nature rhymes

'Pathways Pink'

The pathways were pink, and
The moon held an umbrella
Waiting for the sun to die
And I threw out shrivelled leaves

'Buttons Waiting'

The fixture shadows climbed
The buttons waiting to write
The leaves and flowery rhymes;
For now, I'm sitting in great time

'I Draw a Garland'

On here I draw a garland,
Full of oranges, sweet and
Ripe traced over my shirt
And the *antenna over* the
Moon *looking over* chimneys

'Buttons on my Shirt'

Buttons on my shirt are
Like miniature suns that
Are dressed in white snow
Falling from the blue sky
Hanging the purple moon:

'Curious'

The boughs are curious
In the mist, like fingertips
Stained with roses, lilies,
Red, purple, yellow and
They are compressed by:

'Blue Leaves'

The skies are blue leaves
Turning white as they
Meet the chorus; the
Bud-flower opens to sound

'Song'

The gates are playing
The whitest spiderweb,
Below falling blue leaves
For those turning orange

'Leaves Hang'

The leaves hang over
Me like a corpse on a
Stick—

'Purply Superiors'

From the branches are
Silhouettes creeping up
The lattice; sits the vase
Holding purply superiors

'Oranges'

They threw the oranges
Falling onto the path to
Turn into petals with *verse*

'The Face in the Mirror'

The moon in the sky melted
Onto the clouds like a canvas
Light red, with which I paint
The ghastly face in the mirror

'Fresh Fruits'

The sun lays under its blanket
Decomposing over the baskets
Hanging, are full of fresh fruits
Playing this verse, like the flute

'The Leaves are White'

Hanging in the night
The leaves are white
Like chalk on a string
Washed away, *stream*

The leaf on the web
In the day, is moving,
Turning into a blanket
Was the sun in the clouds

'Cotton Sheet'

Nighttime's blackboard
Had a scythe, and a star
Held up by light boughs
To be left with cuts, scars
Placed over, *cotton sheet*

'Away the Winter Weather'

The branches sing a song,
For the leaves they shake
Away the winter weather—

'Miniature Skulls'

The snow on the bough
Hanging miniature skulls
Dropping onto the leaves
Became green for whites

'Miniature Fruits'

I collect miniature fruits
For the webs, to be
Threaded onto the moon,
Branches in windowpanes

'Snow Like Needles'

The snow fell
Down on me like needles
For nature's rhyme—

'Golden Lockets'

The moon is a white petal
Sleeping on sky-blue paper
Falling from the silver airs
The sun like golden lockets

'The Daytime'

The twigs over the moon:
Scarred by this afternoon

'The Sun on my Finger'

The sun is on my finger
Like a locket, swinging,
From side to side

'Curtains'

The moon behind curtains
On which I draw the night,
I get to touch white flowers
Morning's blue wrist lowers

'The Trees I Climb'

The moon opens its jacket
And welcomes, zips me up
The trees I climb for fruits

'Hanging Warm'

Parentheses held the fruit,
By which I was impressed
The strawberry, that smiled
And the bricks welcomed
The twigs, danced like ghosts
In the moon, hanging *warm*

'Moonspun Flowers'

Moonspun flowers
In the sun, a reality
Wherein they dance

'The Cherry Flakes'

The half-woven moon
Giving off plum-scent
Brings forth an orange,
Come the cherry flakes!

'Apples Bouncing'

On the ellipsis,
Are apples bouncing
Towards the sunshine

'The Moon in Pyjamas'

Chopped bananas,
The moon in pyjamas
Have grass on them

'Musky Melons'

Musky melons are
Cut into halves, but
Dew-laden leaves,
Do make a fine scarf

'I Make a River'

For this sun, in its
Yellow raincoat and
In the dusk floats like
A hand-made boat
Put together, paper

'The Night'

Hanging in *the night*
The leaves are white
Like the fullest moon
Dripping from my chin

'The Moon on my Finger'

The spider on the web
I exchange for threads
So I can stitch together
The moon on my finger

'Weave'

Using my pinkie finger
I weave strawberries
Around the great sun,
For the moon is asleep

'Little Red'

Walking the *path was*
Little Red, swarmed
In leaves *dark-brown*

'My Sock!'

The incy wincy spider
Crawled back under
The rock, down came
The snow, and did the
Cherries flow, my sock!

'Straw Hat'

On the carriage railway
Walking is the sun in his
Straw hat, on the flower
But I'm here, the bower

'Hedges'

In the hedges was
A black cat running
The birds humming
The moon punching
Its moonlight, so red

'A Crop in the Moon'

The harvest was done:
And a crop, in the moon
Smiling, hanging orange,
Peeling off its own skin

'The Cherries in Flight'

The hedge in dusk
Is froze during dawn
Is black in the winter,
The cherries in flight

'Ten Witches'

There are ten witches
On this British moon
With their broomsticks
Sending him to sleep—

'So Bloody Red'

I stick spikes in strawberries
For them to bleed their juice
I can use to paint the canvas
My little finger is so bloody red

'A Hat'

I fold the sun and make
A hat, walking the streets,
Scaring away the black cat

'The Afternoon'

Golden kisses the afternoon
And the moon, gasps for breath,
Earth in blissful twilight:

'Mildewed Moon'

In the night, the blight
Disappears from leaves
I paint them all anaemic
But the mildewed moon:

'The Tree Again'

Out of the moon I make
A paper plane, to throw at,
And swallow, *the tree again*

'Mildewed Fruits'

The tree in tonight's moon
Hanging its fresh fruits:
Grapes, lemons, apples,
All of them, are mildewed

'Frosty White Coats'

The apples falling,
The cherries snoring
In frosty white coats

'The Melted Moon'

The sun held a wine glass
Swirling the melted moon
To pour over itself like glue,
A small leaf on the top grew

'Passerby'

I walk along the mud
And on the grass, a thud:
The moon from the sky
Like a big, big, passerby

'Rain'

I dip my finger in rain
To draw over the moon;
I pinch it for good pain,
On this sunny afternoon

'Black Cloak'

I dress the daytime,
A longer, black cloak;
White buttons, falling,
The palm of my hand

'Footprints'

Flowers guard the moon
On the grass, in the noon,
Leafy swirls cover a face,
And footprints are traced

'Pieces'

I cut apart the sun and
Make a dreamcatcher
For my wall, in the night,
And I stick on the pieces

'Poetry'

I cut apart the sun and
It's no longer shining up
The top of the fruity tree,
It is woven into the poetry

'The Sun to Hang'

For a moment fleeting
Leaves were a fine scarf
For the sun to hang with

'Smiling Moon'

There is the smiling moon
For whom I went shopping
The frame with flowers on,
But inside it has *not a face*

'Moon's Big Mouth'

The crops are on fire
So I start to pick them
And stitch them onto
The moon's big mouth

'The Storm'

The storm passes
Leaving cherries
On the floor

'A Thin Branch'

I collect a thin branch,
Tap onto red lampposts
The rain is fine cherries,
The washed windscreen

'Overcome with Rushes'

I am overcome with rushes
In the black—
Cherries fall

'Clarity is everything.
There's "Love" but no ring.
Please pop the question darling.'

Lina Begum

www.ingramcontent.com/pod-product-compliance
Lightning Source LLC
Chambersburg PA
CBHW032000080426
42735CB00007B/459